A Citizen's Guide to
News & Views

Heinemann
LIBRARY

Sean Connolly

www.heinemann.co.uk/library
visit our website to find out more information about **Heinemann Library** books.

To order:
☎ Phone 44 (0) 1865 888066

▤ Send a fax to 44 (0) 1865 314091

 Visit the Heinemann Bookshop at www.heinemann.co.uk/library to browse our catalogue and order online.

First published in Great Britain by Heinemann Library, Halley Court, Jordan Hill, Oxford OX2 8EJ,
a division of Reed Educational and Professional Publishing Ltd.

Heinemann is a registered trademark of Reed Educational & Professional Publishing Limited.

OXFORD MELBOURNE AUCKLAND JOHANNESBURG BLANTYRE GABORONE IBADAN PORTSMOUTH NH (USA) CHICAGO

Designed by M2 Graphic Design
Indexed by Indexing Specialists
Originated by Ambassador Litho Ltd.
Printed in Hong Kong/China

06 05 04 03 02
10 9 8 7 6 5 4 3 2 1

ISBN 0 431 14491 5

British Library Cataloguing in Publication Data
Connolly, Sean, 1956-
A citizen's guide to news and views
1. Mass media - Juvenile literature
2. Mass media - Social aspects - Juvenile literature
I. Title II.News and views
302.2'3

Acknowledgements
The Publishers would like to thank the following for permission to reproduce photgraphs:
Bridgeman Art Library p6; Cern p30; Corbis pp19, 23, 38; Corbis/Reuters p37; Greenpeace p32; Hulton Picture Library p9 (top); Hulton Picture Library/Bettmann Archive p10; ITC p29; John Frost Newspapers p9 (bottom); News International Corporation pp12, 33; PA Photos p21; Popperfoto pp16, 41; Rex Features p24; Thames TV p28; *The Herald* (SMG Newspapers, Glasgow) p34; The *Independent* pp15, 27; Tony Stone p5.

Cover photograph reproduced with permission of Corbis.

Every effort has been made to contact copyright holders of any material reproduced in this book.
Any omissions will be rectified in subsequent printings if notice is given to the Publisher.

CONTENTS

Introduction

What is the media?   4

History

Sending messages   6

The printed word   8

The global perspective   10

The key players

'The Press'   12

Movers and shakers   14

The price of the news   16

Mission to inform   18

On the air   20

Television   22

'One picture is worth...'   24

Further afield   26

Taken to task   28

The Internet   30

Media moguls   32

Britain's role

Regional awareness   34

Northern Ireland – a special case?   36

Whose information?   38

Look to the future

Confusion or clarity?   40

Debate

Issues for discussion   42

Further resources   44

Glossary   46

Index   48

Any words appearing in the text in bold, **like this**, are explained in the Glossary.

INTRODUCTION
What is the media?

At the beginning of the twenty-first century, Britain is learning about itself, using forms of communication that are dramatically different from those that were available as the twentieth century began. It is easy to list the technological advances – in the fields of science, medicine, entertainment and even leisure – that have marked the last hundred years. People live longer, work shorter hours and have access to state-of-the-art facilities that make most tasks easier.

But one area in which this technological progress has been most noticeable, and in some ways most intimidating, has been in what is often described as the 'Information Age'. Loosely speaking, this term refers to the way in which we are constantly bombarded with news from many different sources – newspapers, magazines, television, radio and the Internet. The last three of these channels of information did not even exist a hundred years ago. In the case of the Internet, it is only in your lifetime that it has made its mark, and it is constantly changing and evolving.

Making choices

Newspapers, magazines, radio and television – the forms of communication that are generally known as 'the media' – exist to inform as well as entertain us. And in a **pluralist, democratic** society such as Britain's, these are important tools for helping us to make informed choices about the direction the nation should take. Together they form an intricate network of information, and people are free to choose which of the various media to follow in order to make their minds up about social issues.

The media shapes, and is shaped by, society. It is often said that we 'get the media we deserve' and in most people's eyes, the British media is excellent. Part of this excellence comes from its variety. We are free to choose between catching up on the latest soap star gossip in a **tabloid** newspaper or reading a detailed analysis of the Budget Speech in the *Financial Times.* Similar choices exist in broadcasting, both in radio and television. The British people have a choice of media to use to make their own choices – choices about food, fashion or even government.

A place in society

The Labour Party achieved its overwhelming election victory in 1997 by positioning itself as the party that would take Britain into the new millennium with energy and a fresh attitude. Old slogans and logos were ditched in favour of a new approach that tried to bridge the gap between old divisions, such as class, race and wealth. Some of the language used in the 1997 election campaign has now been dropped by the party, as it has moved from focusing on opposing other political parties to dealing with the practicalities of governing Britain.

A television production team examines the consoles with massed screens and sound feed in order to choose which images are broadcast.

But one term has managed to creep into the different social layers of the country. That term is '**stakeholder**'. Broadly speaking, a stakeholder is someone who has a vested interest in an aspect of society. The term carries with it some suggestion of being responsible for what is happening in society and underpins many of the modern notions of citizenship. A stakeholder might receive a service, but he or she can also shape that service. The British people are also stakeholders in the media that informs us about our country.

This book tells the story of the media and explains the effect that print, broadcast and electronic media have on us as citizens. Certain themes run through this story, providing glimpses of the qualities that the British most value in themselves. Freedom of speech, of course, is important in our history, and many people see the Internet as the ultimate provider of this democratic right. But just as important are the values of compromise and tolerance. Britain, unlike many other countries, has never had a state-controlled media system, and not many people would welcome increased government control over what we hear, see or read. But in a time when media empires are built and sustained with vast fortunes, individuals can come to have the sort of powers that the British have always denied their governments. This book looks to the future of the media, which is likely to be shaped by the lessons of the past.

FIND OUT...

The British Broadcasting Corporation (BBC) has a unique place in Britain's media. If we use a television, we have to buy a licence. The licence fee goes to fund the BBC. Find out more about the BBC and its funding on its website at www.bbc.co.uk/info.

HISTORY
Sending messages

During the Middle Ages, the monarch's (a king or queen) means of communication with his or her people was very different to how it is now. Apart from the large cities such as London and Bristol, settlements were scattered and it was difficult to travel long distances. The only 'publications' that were relevant and of immediate concern to the whole population existed to reinforce the country's two institutions of authority: the monarchy and the Church. The Domesday Book, compiled in 1086, and Magna Carta, dating from 1215, are two major examples of public documents. Only a few copies of each would have existed, and the overall understanding of these documents would have come to 'ordinary' citizens through noblemen and land owners.

There were two important reasons for this selective distribution of documents. Most important is the fact the overwhelming proportion of the population could not read or write. It would be pointless trying to distribute large numbers of written documents to people whose lives revolved around the change of seasons and whose routines were imposed by farming. The second reason was that every document needed to be handwritten. People known as scribes needed to spend all the daylight hours making detailed copies of each document.

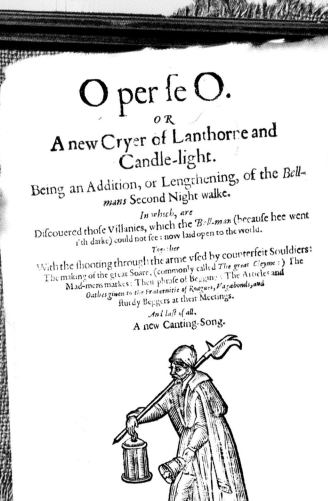

O per fe O.
OR
A new Cryer of Lanthorre and Candle-light.

Being an Addition, or Lengthening, of the Bellmans Second Night walke.

In which, are
Difcouered thofe Villanies, which the Bell-man (becaufe hee went i'th darke) could not fee : now laid open to the world.

Together
With the fhooting through the arme vfed by counterfeit Souldiers: The making of the great Soare, (commonly called The great Cleyme :) The Mad-mens markes : Then phrafe of Begging : The Articles and Oathes given to the Fraternitie of Roagues, Vagabonds, and fturdy Beggers at their Meetings.

And laft of all,
A new Canting-Song.

Printed at London for Iohn Bufbie, and are to be fould at his fhop in S. Dunftans Church-yard in Fleete-ftreet. 1 6 1 2.

The Church

Most scribes, in fact, worked within the structure of the medieval church. The Church offered one of the few routes to increasing a person's intellectual knowledge, as well as being the main 'employer' of those who could read and write. But the Church was preoccupied with the breakdown of social structures that had signalled the start of what were later called the Dark Ages. Traditional routes of knowledge had been disrupted by the fall of the Roman Empire and two centuries later by the rise of Islam in the Holy Lands and beyond.

The Church relied on imposing its own strict social structure and the corresponding system of religious practices for believers. Informing the public about late-breaking news – which would probably lead to unsettling questions being asked – was not a priority. Instead, the Church's scribes devoted themselves to copying ancient books of knowledge. Topical documents, such as the Pope's command for the various Crusades, would be read out at Mass on Sunday, and probably interpreted in a simpler fashion for the public.

A sixteenth-century flysheet looks back at the role of the town crier – soon to become a figure of history with the introduction of printing.

The public at large

Although the public lived in self-contained hamlets and towns, profound events did occur which needed to be made known across the kingdom. News of royal visits, battles and sessions of Parliament would reach each corner of England, usually by means of messengers on horseback. Again, the news would be generated by – and supportive of – authority. Signal flares and beacons offered a visual explanation for emergencies, and at a very local level the town crier might add an element of local news to his calls.

But within this period one major change occurred that would pave the way for knowledge to be more widely spread throughout the country. It was hardly noticed by the public at first, having more of an immediate effect on the scribes working for King and Church. That development was the introduction of paper in the eleventh century. Paper had been invented in China and was brought back to Europe by travelling merchants. In its own way, this material was revolutionary, as it was far less expensive to produce and maintain than **parchment**. It could also be stored and transported with ease. The real breakthrough would come in the fifteenth century, with the introduction of the printing press.

HISTORY
The printed word

Medieval thought, in Britain as elsewhere in Europe, underwent an enormous change from about the fourteenth century onwards. At stake was the view, held for more than a millennium, that human beings were somehow destined to serve authority, either in the form of the monarchy or the Church. Ideas that came to be known generally as humanism – that the individual has value beyond serving authority – developed alongside the artistic revolution known as the **Renaissance**.

The new ideas, however, were accessible only to the intellectual elite and the economically powerful – people who could afford the time and money to read the new documents that made their way through Europe. Two major events, which are often linked in history books, blew apart the medieval **consensus**. The first was the invention of the printing press. The second, which could only develop through the distribution of printed documents, was the Protestant **Reformation**. The printing press was developed by Johann Gutenburg in Germany in 1450. Individual blocks, each containing one letter, were be fitted neatly on to a plate. After this basic preparation, a printer could run off hundreds of copies of a page quite easily. Printing presses became common throughout Europe by about 1500, leading in the major social upheavals of the sixteenth and seventeenth centuries.

Spreading the word

Affordable bibles, printed in the language of the people rather than in Latin (the language of the Roman Catholic Church), were the ammunition that religious reformers used during the turbulent sixteenth century. The public, regardless of their political or religious beliefs, became intrigued with readily available reading material. Hand in hand with the bibles were other religious texts, such as those used by the **Puritan** movement in order to press for changes within the Church of England.

It did not take long for governments – and those who secretly opposed them – to recognize the power of the printed word. In the late sixteenth century and early seventeenth century a number of publications, known as *corrants* (loosely translated as 'current' or 'current events'), developed on the Continent. Usually confined to one page, the *corrants* dealt with political issues of the day – sometimes a single issue dominated the whole page. By the 1620s, English-language versions of the *corrants* were available in England, but it was only in 1641, with the abolition of the Star Chamber (in effect, a royal censorship office), that England saw its own newspapers develop.

Events in Parliament were first reported in 1641, in the *Diurnall occurrences in Parliament*. This was a basic report on the debates of the day, with little effort at adding a political point of view. But with the English Civil War on the horizon, both Parliamentary and Royalist groups began to use newspapers to try to influence public opinion.

Hard-won freedom

The continental and English newspapers were not the first publications to present news to the public. More than 1600 years before, ancient Rome had its own version known as the *Acta Diurna* (Daily Events). In the first century BC, Julius Caesar ordered these handwritten news bulletins to be posted each day in the Forum. And the first printed newspaper, produced from wood blocks, had appeared in Beijing, China, in the seventh or eighth century AD.

But these early versions, like their seventeenth-century counterparts, were strictly controlled. There was no notion of a '**free press**' in mid-seventeenth-century England, and after Parliament's victory in the Civil War, Oliver Cromwell imposed harsh restrictions on the press. The Licensing Act that Cromwell revived suppressed all newspapers except official publications. One of these, the *Oxford Gazette*, was founded in 1665 and became the *London Gazette* in 1666. It remains the world's oldest surviving **periodical**.

It was only after William III came to the throne in 1689 that the press received some of the freedom that it now enjoys. The Licensing Act fell into disuse in 1679, and in its wake came a flood of new publications. These could still be closed by the Government, but in 1695 Parliament voted against renewing the Licensing Act.

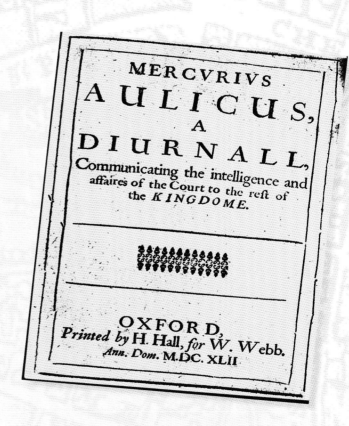

The mid-seventeenth-century Royalist version of events appeared in the pages of the *Mercurius Aulicus*. Opposing these views was the Parliamentary *Mercurius Britannicus*.

FIND OUT...

The *London Gazette* is the official newspaper of the Crown. This edition dates from February 26, 1684. You can have a look at it online at www.london-gazette.co.uk You can also find out about the Scottish *Edinburgh Gazette* and the Northern Irish *Belfast Gazette*.

HISTORY
The global perspective

The eighteenth century saw England – and Britain as a whole – entering a period of relative peace and prosperity. With the internal upheavals of the previous century largely resolved, the country concentrated on building an international trading empire, with the military force to defend its gains. The political health of the country was also in good shape, given a new energy by the mix of newspapers that had sprung up to support the new political parties.

The journalism of the period was mainly political; journalism was regarded as an extension of politics, and each political group had its own newspaper. It was during this period that the great British journalists flourished, among them Daniel Defoe, Jonathan Swift, Sir Richard Steele and Joseph Addison.

The great dailies

It is within this period of economic prosperity and lively intellectual debate that the seeds of modern journalism were sown. By the late eighteenth century, newspapers had shown themselves to be not simply mouthpieces for political opinion, but potential money-spinners as well. On 1 January 1785, John Walter founded the *Daily Universal Register*, which became *The Times* exactly three years later, now Britain's oldest surviving newspaper with continuous daily publication.

Other elements of what we would see as the modern newspaper industry were falling into place at around the same time. In 1788, the *Star and Evening Advertiser* became the first daily evening newspaper.

Just two years later the *Sunday Chronicle* became the first Sunday morning newspaper, with its 4am publication time. Other Sunday newspapers followed the *Chronicle's* lead by publishing early on a Sunday morning instead of on Saturday night. The year 1791 saw the first issue of the *Observer*, which is Britain's oldest surviving Sunday newspaper.

Fleet Street

London, like other major cities, has streets or districts that are linked with a certain profession. Harley Street means first-class doctors and surgeons, whilst Saville Row is the centre of men's tailoring. But none of these familiar streets can match Fleet Street, which for nearly two centuries was Britain's newspaper industry, or so it seemed. For many people the words 'Fleet Street' have become synonymous with newspaper journalism, so much so that we still hear it in phrases such as 'Fleet Street responded to the Prince's request...'

It all began in 1815, when the *Morning Advertiser*, founded by the Licensed **Victuallers** Association, became the first daily to be published in Fleet Street. Other titles, including the *Telegraph* and the *Standard*, started up nearby. Close proximity meant that they could benefit from news agencies such as Reuters, which opened in 1851. Reporters could 'network' in the Fleet Street pubs; owners benefited by learning of the competition's 'scoops'. Similar press districts formed in Manchester, Glasgow and Edinburgh.

The modern era

Newspapers and magazines dealing with news and opinion, such as the *Spectator*, soon realized that new technology meant more readers. The first newspaper illustrations appeared in 1806 and the first photographs appeared in 1889.

The big changes came in the twentieth century with the appearance of radio and television. Only radio existed when the British Broadcasting Company (later **Corporation**) was founded in 1922. Under the bold and sometimes **authoritarian** leadership of its first Director General, John Reith, the BBC set about establishing a threefold purpose for broadcasting: to educate, entertain and to inform.

Television arrived in Britain about three decades after radio, and it, too, was subjected to strict regulations about its content and aims. Initially, the BBC had a **monopoly** on all television broadcasts, but commercially driven (that is, relying on advertising) television arrived in the 1950s. The Independent Television Commission (ITC) was formed to act as a similar 'watchdog' for commercial television.

The late twentieth century saw the arrival of the Internet, with its much-praised free flow of ideas. As we more further into the new Millennium, it is becoming harder to see how the three more 'traditional' media – print journalism, radio and television – will respond to the competition posed by the Net.

Old-style printing: teams of typesetters assemble the blocks of print, letter by letter, at a London newspaper in about 1910.

THE KEY PLAYERS
'The Press'

When we talk about 'the Press', we mean all the newspapers and magazines that are published. The phrase is often used to talk about only the newspapers and magazines that report news and reflect public opinion.

The **free press** has long been one of Britain's most cherished traditions. The public expects reporters and columnists to expose the weaknesses as well as the strengths of the people in power. Newspapers, political magazines and more academic publications set about doing just that, reflecting a range of opinions among both writers and readers. However, not all of the newspapers available on news-stands are devoted to serious analysis of topical issues; many of the most popular titles are far more concerned with show business, sports and gossip.

'Quality' versus popularity

A British opinion that has applied for decades is that the size of a newspaper reflects its relative seriousness. Larger size equals more in-depth analysis, as well as a style of writing that assumes that its reader has a reasonable amount of knowledge.

>> **Broadsheets**: Five national daily newspapers fit this description – *The Times, Daily Telegraph, Independent, Guardian, Financial Times*. They are published in the format known as

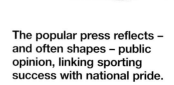

The popular press reflects – and often shapes – public opinion, linking sporting success with national pride.

broadsheet. A typical issue might have two or more separate sections – covering related topics such as main news, culture, sport and fashion – printed in this large format, and slipped inside each other.

>> **Tabloids:** Representing the opposite end of the 'size equals quality' spectrum are the tabloids, such as the *Sun, Mirror, Star* and *Daily Sport*. The tabloid format produces newspapers that are roughly half the size of broadsheets – small enough to be displayed in full, rather than folded in half horizontally. As a rule, the balance between words and pictures is weighed more heavily towards pictures in tabloids. Consequently, articles are much shorter than those in the broadsheets. The tabloid versus broadsheet divide is also evident in the choice of Sunday newspapers in Britain.

The differences between broadsheet and tabloid newspapers are far more profound than just the technical differences discussed above, touching on issues such as educational achievement, political bias, honest reporting and popularity. Supporters of broadsheet newspapers accept that tabloids are more popular: the average tabloid sells more than six times as many copies as the average broadsheet. But, say the critics of tabloids, this popularity comes at a cost to journalistic integrity. In catering to the taste for gossip in their readers and by devoting themselves to entertaining, the tabloids reduce the scope for presentation of hard facts.

Those who work on tabloid newspapers have a different story to tell. In their view, broadsheets indulge their writers far too much, running lengthy pieces of analysis that frequently become bogged down in 'On the one hand...on the other' style of writing. Tabloid journalists also maintain that rather than lacking detailed analysis, their work requires a far greater skill in **encapsulating** the main points of a news story. The *Financial Times,* for example, will print large sections of, for example, the Chancellor's annual Budget Speech. These can run to several thousand words. The *Mirror*, for reasons of space, will produce 200–300 words about the speech, outlining the main aspects that relate to their readers. It takes enormous skill to digest the speech and produce a concise analysis. Each newspaper caters to the demands and expectations of its reader.

Magazines

In addition to the wide range of daily and Sunday newspapers, Britain has a variety of magazines that reflect and often help shape public and political opinion. The most influential, including the *Spectator*, *New Statesman and Society* and *The Economist*, are weeklies. The magazine sector expects as much, or more, of its readers as the broadsheets, and the pages are full of detailed analysis as well as in-depth stories on items that might pop up simply as news items in the newspapers. *The Economist*, like its nearest counterparts in the United States (*Time* and *Newsweek*), has no acknowledged political 'line'. Others are more direct in their support of a political party or philosophy. The *Spectator* has traditionally supported the Conservative Party, while *New Statesman and Society* more often supports Labour.

In addition to news reporting and analysis, aims shared by newspapers, magazines spend time and effort in exposing corruption and hypocrisy in high places. The leading publication in this respect is the fortnightly *Private Eye*, which devotes itself more or less evenly between **satirical** articles and exposures of scandalous behaviour.

FIND OUT...

Have a look at a range of newspapers and magazines. Compare articles on similar subjects in *The Times* and the *Sun* or the *Daily Mirror*. Most newspapers and magazines now have online editions. Try visiting some of their websites. Here are a few to start with: www.thesun.co.uk, www.mirror.co.uk, www.thetimes.co.uk www.independent.co.uk.

THE KEY PLAYERS
Movers and shakers

Although most newspapers are prepared to meet the task of supplying late-breaking information, the core of their work depends much more on forward planning and discussion. 'Choice' is almost certainly the most important word in the decision-making that goes into deciding how an edition will look. This means that, following the guidance of its editor, a newspaper will decide where and how to make the best use of its forces.

The editor presides over a collection of departments, which, for daily newspapers, are still known as '**desks**'. Each of these desks has its own editor. There is a general allocation of pages to each desk, and the running order remains constant with each edition, largely to make the regular reader feel familiar with the newspaper. Generally, the front page, which in effect sells the paper to undecided readers, contains elements of the most important stories from each desk. The inside of the paper conforms to a set pattern of pages.

Look more closely at any newspaper, and you will see how the finished product is divided among these various desks:

>> Front page gives the Headline News – what the paper considers to be the main news of the day. In a **broadsheet** paper, this will usually be a political story or a major disaster. **Tabloid** papers will often give their front page over to a story about a film or TV star.

>> Home News usually runs from page two for anything between four and eight pages.

>> Foreign News normally gets less coverage than Home News.

>> Financial News – London-based dailies refer to the Financial News section as the 'city desk' in reference to the City of London.

>> Sport is almost always at the end of the paper.

The other main daily sections are Arts and the Leader/Feature page, which deals with analysis of the latest news as well as offering opinions and letters to the editor. Many papers have sections that appear only once a week – for example, Media, Computing, Science.

Making the choices

An editor has at his or her disposal a team of specialists: reporters (both foreign-based and domestic), feature writers, photographers and illustrators backed up by a picture library, and teams of sub-editors whose job it is to make the 'copy' (text and content) read sensibly and fit within an allocated space.

All newspapers and political magazines have regular editorial meetings in which newsworthy stories are discussed. Then the editor and his or her team will put together a 'rough' of the next edition, suggesting space allocation and likely pictures. Reporters, who tend to work within one department only, might be sent to pursue stories that have been discussed.

It is in the field of domestic political reporting that the press relies on insiders' leaks, 'off the record' remarks and other unofficial means of obtaining information. The Government publishes dozens of press briefings, but simply repeating what is written in these official documents carries less weight than something that a reporter has learnt based on hard-won personal contact with senior figures. This unofficial approach to disclosing news is well accepted by central government in Westminster and carries its own unspoken rules, collectively known as the Lobby System.

The Lobby System

Journalists who are allowed to frequent the Members' Lobby and other restricted areas within the Houses of Parliament are able to find out information that is denied to other reporters. This information, which might be termed 'official leaks', is offered with the understanding that the reporters are not allowed to disclose the source.

This system benefits both the journalists and those who are providing the information. The journalists may find their jobs made easier by being provided with a steady flow of inside information, gossip and opinion. The senior politicians and civil servants, on the other hand, can lessen the blow of potentially unpleasant news, such as bad unemployment figures, so that the stock market will not react badly when the news is released officially a few days later. The secret element of the information also allows senior officials, and even **Cabinet** members, to sneak in opinions that go against Government policy.

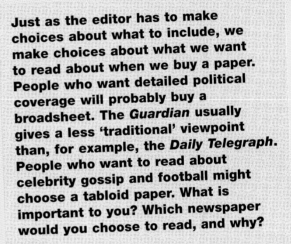

FIND OUT...

Just as the editor has to make choices about what to include, we make choices about what we want to read about when we buy a paper. People who want detailed political coverage will probably buy a broadsheet. The *Guardian* usually gives a less 'traditional' viewpoint than, for example, the *Daily Telegraph*. People who want to read about celebrity gossip and football might choose a tabloid paper. What is important to you? Which newspaper would you choose to read, and why?

Former Conservative leader William Hague is shown here, surrounded by journalists, in an 'off-the-cuff' speech.

THE KEY PLAYERS
The price of the news

'I read it in the papers, so it must be true.' Most people will react with a laugh on hearing these words, but it is worth asking why. Just what is it that makes most people feel that a newspaper has its own opinion? And if the truth is given a new angle in this way, whose interests are served, and how is the Press restricted by what it writes?

Newspapers and magazines live or die on the money they receive from **circulation** and advertising revenue. Each publication strikes a balance between these sources of income: at the two extremes are '**freesheets**' which survive on advertising income alone, and learned journals, which rely on circulation to survive. Financial realities – driven by either advertising or circulation concerns – act as a brake on papers including too much controversial material that might lose them either advertisers or readers.

Related to this concern is the whole notion of newspaper (and magazine) ownership. In the heyday of Fleet Street in the early twentieth century, newspaper 'barons' owned many major titles, exercising exclusive power over the look and content of their papers. Editors would know enough

Rupert Murdoch (left) conferring with MPs Robin Cook (right) and Mark Fisher (centre) at the 1998 European Audiovisual Conference.

not to run stories that might offend an owner's political or social opinions. Even today, Rupert Murdoch's News International is the leading player in the ownership stakes. Murdoch's company owns *The Times* and the *Sunday Times* – both **broadsheets** – as well as the leading daily **tabloids** the *Sun* and the *News of the World*. These papers, combined with powerful interests in broadcasting, give Murdoch a role that even the most influential of the earlier press barons would envy. Neither have his papers been shy about reflecting their owner's views. Influence such as this extends beyond shaping public opinion – it puts strong pressure on public officials if they are not to face a great deal of bad publicity.

The law

The reluctance of editors to publish stories that might be damaging in financial or personal career terms amounts to a kind of self-censorship. In theory, the decision not to run certain stories is freely taken. Courageous or simply skilful editors can go against the opinions of their **proprietors**, but usually retain their jobs only if sales figures justify the chance taken. But publications face other important constraints, both of which can land editors in a court of law.

The first involves censorship originating at Government level. Newspapers can therefore be brought to trial for disclosing information that was considered vital to national security.

Far more common, however, are those cases that are brought about by an individual. These cases, almost always centring on interpretations of the **libel** laws, can draw huge publicity, and the damages awarded can threaten the financial security of a publication if it is found guilty.

The Press Complaints Commission, a voluntary non-governmental board, listens to accusations of press bias or inaccuracy, and sometimes offers stern criticism to editors whom it considers have breached the rules of **ethics**. Libel actions, on the other hand, are expensive and time-consuming, usually beyond the reach of the ordinary person. Some senior politicians and business people, however, have become famous for their libel actions.

In addition to the financial awards that go to a successful libel **plaintiff**, the guilty publication is usually forced to print some form of apology or retraction. It is common for both parties to reach an out-of-court settlement, also linked to some form of payment and apology. Richard Ingrams, former editor of *Private Eye*, would often get around these settlements by publishing apologies that were so remorseful that any reader could see that they were not really meant.

> **'At a later stage in the Maxwell (libel case) cross-examination, Mr Hartley asked me whether I had ever published anything in *Private Eye* which I knew to be untrue. Yes, I replied, the apologies.'**
>
> (Former *Private Eye* editor Richard Ingrams quoted in *The Penguin Book of Journalism*)

THE KEY PLAYERS
Mission to inform

The press has been subject to a system of checks and balances, controls, voluntary guidelines and forms of legal **redress** for centuries. New cases sometimes establish legal precedents, but really, both publisher and reader are subject to the same legal position that existed in the past. The twentieth century, however, saw the start of an era of diversity and possibly **anarchy** with the advent of broadcasting. New systems of monitoring and quality control of the media became necessary, and as the twenty-first century arrived, these systems showed signs of continuing to change to keep pace with technological developments.

In its original meaning, 'broadcasting' meant sowing grains by casting seeds across a wide area. This is a very suitable image for the modern use of the word. Broadcasting in its simplest terms refers to the transmission and reception of radio or television signals. Radio transmissions from a single station are often broadcast over several **wavelengths**, and most radios are able to pick up signals on all of these wavelengths, or bands. Traditional television broadcasts, beamed out and received along broadly similar lines to those of radio, are now termed '**terrestrial** broadcasts'. This is to distinguish them from transmissions beamed off satellites, which can only be received through a special 'dish'. Cable television, in which the signals arrive through fibre-optic cables connected to a building, also represent a departure from terrestrial broadcasts.

Seeking order

Radio was the test case that laid the foundations of the broadcasting arrangements that still govern Britain. As radio technology developed in the early 1920s, it became obvious that the British Government, and society as a whole, should come to some sort of agreement about the aims and potential of broadcasting. Variations of some of the early arguments can still be heard today. Some people argued that broadcasting should be as uncluttered by restrictions – in particular, government restrictions – as possible. This 'free market' approach would allow stations to spring up almost freely, with the authorization to broadcast more or less what they chose, and to broadcast commercially. At the other end of the spectrum, there were those who felt that this powerful medium was too important to be left in the hands of anyone with enough money to set up a station. In effect, they were arguing for the strictest form of government investigation, if not outright control.

The result of these debates was a compromise, but one that has held the respect of all major political parties. The British Broadcasting Company (later

Corporation) was set up in 1922. Its aim was to set up broadcasting as a public service **monopoly**; the audience members were to be treated as citizens rather than consumers. In this way, from the start, the BBC set about to educate the public to play more of a role in the political and cultural life of the nation. Under its first Director-General, John Reith, the BBC aimed to educate, entertain and inform. This same thinking underpinned the setting up, in succession, of each new BBC radio station (both local and national) and television channel.

The broadcasting structure

The BBC is run by a Director-General and his or her management team, who is in turn answerable to the BBC Board of Governors under a chairman chosen by the Home Secretary. Although there is a political air to this last position, the BBC guards its independence from Government fiercely, and its funding comes from the licence fees that the public pay.

This system also played a part in the establishment of the Independent Television Commission (ITC), which acts as a safeguard in relation to commercial television broadcasting. Independent television is financed by advertising that runs during and after programmes. Its output is created by fifteen separate programme companies, each of which has a **franchise** to broadcast in a certain part of the country. ITV franchises run for an agreed period on contract (usually ten years) and are subject to investigation and competition – in terms of quality and overall output – when the time comes for a contract to be renewed. Similar franchises operate in commercial local radio.

The BBC sets out clear aims for its two television channels: BBC 1 tends to cater to the widest possible audience, while BBC 2 can provide programmes with a more cultural and educational basis. Therefore, it is the obvious home of Open University programmes. The main ITV channel roughly equals BBC1 in its overall framework; Channel 4 came into being to provide BBC 2-style broadcasting within the commercial sector. Channel 5, the newest independent channel, is another 'popular' channel.

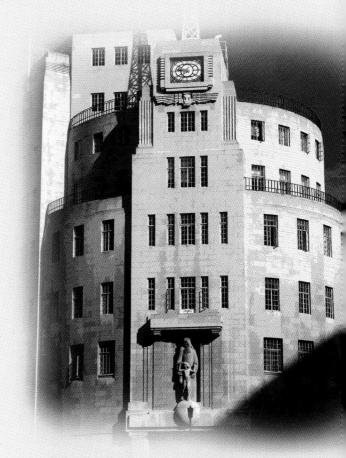

Broadcasting house in west London is the headquarters of the BBC.

THE KEY PLAYERS
On the air

With the development of radio in the early twentieth century, the word 'media' began to appear. It would later come to suggest a complex variety of meanings, but at the outset the word was taken at face value – as the plural of the word 'medium'. The BBC's aims from the start tied in with this earlier meaning. In its view, transmitting via radio (the earliest broadcasting medium) was very much like sowing seeds – the seeds of ideas and opinions within the general listening public.

More than 75 years after the first BBC radio broadcasts in 1924, the 'brief' for radio broadcasting has become much wider. Three-quarters of a century ago it would have been hard to imagine 'gangsta' rap, swearing and phone-in sex counselling coming from the radio. But these elements now form part of a diverse broadcasting environment. The commitment to the arts, political analysis (the 'Today' programme) and wide-ranging musical tastes (festivals such as Glastonbury being broadcast on Radio 1, and nearly all of the Radio 3 output) is as strong as ever.

One programme on BBC Radio 4 is considered the UK's most important current affairs radio programme. 'Today' attracts an audience of just over 2 million. This is a relatively small figure compared to many TV programmes but it includes many of the country's most powerful people. 10 Downing Street records the whole programme every morning.

BBC National radio

The BBC operates five national radio stations, each with its own intended audience. Radio 1 is the popular music station, periodically undergoing changes to keep its youthful appeal. Radio 2, for many years considered an unfashionable 'easy listening' backwater, has now attracted many 'baby boomer' listeners and presenters for its mix of popular music and features aimed at a slightly older listening public. Radio 3 is known for playing 'serious' music, and it sometimes includes features on jazz or world music. Radio 4 is the first of two 'speech-only' stations, supplying a variety of news, political and cultural analysis and drama. 5 Live, the newest of the BBC national stations, offers a mix of live sporting broadcasts and studio discussions and phone-ins.

The World Service is a branch of the BBC that is aimed at foreign listeners. Its mission is to offer listeners a radio 'snapshot' of life in Britain, as well as to provide an internationally respected source of news. World Service broadcasts are a mix of BBC material from the other five stations, as well as original broadcasts in many foreign languages.

Commercial radio

Commercial radio developed in the late 1960s, at about the same time that the BBC responded to offshore (non-British-based) 'pirate' stations beaming in the sort of pop music that was not generally available on the BBC. As a result, the first commercial stations also catered to this pop music market, and today most commercial stations still concentrate on music. The big difference now is that listening audiences have become more fragmented, and stations often concentrate on capturing just one segment of the listening public – pitching their 'playlists' towards soul, jazz and blues 'golden oldies' and so on. Commercial stations are also almost all locally based, so that advertising and public service announcements are aimed at a local listenership.

The Radio Authority licenses and regulates all non-BBC radio broadcasting – in effect, commercial radio – in the United Kingdom. The biggest recent development in commercial radio has been the licensing of national commercial stations – Classic FM, Virgin and Talk Sport. Provided that listening figures remain high, more licences for national commercial stations will follow.

Local radio

When BBC Radio first went on air in 1924, there were twenty **low-power stations**. Because of the limits of transmission power, these were all local stations. Within a few years, however, the BBC was able to upgrade its transmissions and the national networks emerged, at the expense of local broadcasting on the BBC. Things changed in the 1960s, however, with the establishment of city-based stations, beginning with Radio Leicester in 1967. Today there are 37 local BBC stations serving England and the Channel Islands, and regional and community radio services in Scotland, Wales and Northern Ireland.

Although monitored by a Managing Director of Regional Broadcasting, each station manager has complete control over the running of the station, and the local radio stations all have the BBC news-gathering resources at their disposal at no cost. Travel, weather and essential information must be tailored to the individual community. This also means that significant ethnic minorities within the local area must be catered for.

Prime Minister Tony Blair is shown here being interviewed on London radio, Choice FM by news editor Pam Joseph.

THE KEY PLAYERS
Television

Television is perhaps the most important source of information within Britain. It is also the most popular leisure pastime:

>> 95 per cent of all households have a colour television set

>> 68 per cent (just over two-thirds) of households also have a video recorder

>> On average there are about two television sets per household. This figure has almost doubled since 1970.

This gives television unequalled influence over the public. Unlike some European countries where the government plays an active role in the choice and approval of programming, British television broadcasting – in the same way as radio broadcasting – is free of government involvement. There are some people who believe that the BBC is somehow a 'highbrow' state-sponsored organization, but the **Corporation** jealously guards its independence and has often been at the receiving end of fierce government criticism.

Setting the issue of state control aside, however, the BBC does have a reputation for being 'nannyish'. This reputation, which took root in the 1950's but is now slowly being broken down, is probably a carry-over from the radio era – in particular during the war years when the BBC's role as a morale builder was invaluable. The BBC nickname, 'Aunty', reflects this image of a well-meaning but slightly fussy superior who always knows best. The BBC at times finds itself seen as old-fashioned, and the idea that it is controlled by 'chaps in suits' is an accusation it must address. Perhaps the strongest critics of the 'public good' role of the BBC (and to an extent, the ITC) are those who favour a more detached approach to broadcasting, usually with the underlying motive of getting rid of regulations to maximize profits. But used skilfully, these arguments can be presented as improving output by tying in with the strong anti-censorship views expressed in certain quarters of the quality press. The result is that the goal of relatively regulation-free competition has become part of the political fabric in Britain. Some of its strongest supporters are within the Labour Party, which has traditionally opposed **deregulation**.

Competition and varied goals

The BBC has actually entered the new Millennium with an awareness of the fierce competition it faces in the television market. The 'duopoly' it enjoyed for decades – competing with, but sharing the audience with ITV – has ended. Competition has come from various fronts, including the multi-channel alternatives offered by satellite and **digital** broadcasting.

'Who Wants to be a Millionaire?' is as popular now in Canada as it is in the UK.

Faced with the demands of public service and competition, British broadcasters must be able to win critics and draw in viewers. Successful programmes also work as important revenue earners for both the BBC and ITV. Versions of 'Who Wants to be a Millionaire?' have appeared in many different countries, and successful entertainment programmes (for example, 'Inspector Morse' and 'S Club 7') are sold to dozens of other countries. But in order for these programmes to reach export-earner status, they must prove themselves first with the British public.

FIND OUT...

Both the BBC and ITV aim to compile accurate indications of how many households watch their programmes as well as how highly the audience rates them. ITV does this because of the same commercial concerns that underpin surveys of newspaper and magazine readership, and radio listening figures. Quite simply, advertisers want to know whether they are getting value (translated as millions of viewers) for their money. The BBC needs to know whether its programmes are 'pulling their weight' (attracting large enough audiences) to justify spending licence fee money on them. To provide the data, the BBC and ITV work together in the Broadcasters' Audience Research Board Limited. The method of finding out viewing figures is to monitor the viewing patterns of a carefully selected group of three thousand homes. These households are chosen in order to provide a miniature version of the country as a whole, in terms of geographical distribution, income, urban versus rural setting and so forth. Electronic meters are attached to the television sets and register when the set is turned on and off, and which channel is being watched. In addition, a similar sample of households regularly fill in questionnaire booklets, in which they rate programmes in terms of popularity. You can find out what people watch on TV by visiting the Broadcasters' Audience Research Board website at www.barb.co.uk. Ratings are also printed regularly in national newspapers.

THE KEY PLAYERS
'One picture is worth...'

Political success depends on what has often been described as 'the oxygen of publicity', and nowhere is this publicity as instantaneous and as widespread than on television. Ministers and their shadow **Cabinet** counterparts know that a high profile is necessary for their success, and their parties recognize the need to increase public awareness of their strategies. Politicians use two methods to achieve this publicity:

>> Making use of the broadcast slots automatically allocated to politics. Three main parties have slots allocated to them for party political broadcasts, increasing around Budget time and in the run-up to General Elections. Since Parliament became televized in the late 1980s, all the major parties have ensured that their spokesmen are seen in highlights. Parliament seems almost deserted at times, so the parties use a ploy called 'doughnutting'. Members wander from their normal seats to surround a fellow member being filmed (like a ring doughnut around its hole), giving a misleading appearance of political support.

>> Parliamentary and party political broadcasts, however, are notoriously unpopular with viewers, so the parties also use the 'unofficial' route of 'spin'. Politically, this term refers to putting a gloss or favourable angle on the party's stance on a particular issue, usually in a short interview during a television news broadcast. Bearing in mind that a particular politician might only be on screen for a few seconds, he or she needs to come up with a catchy phrase – a **'sound bite'** – that sums up party policy and sticks in the public mind.

The then Labour Party leader Neil Kinnock was caught unaware and tripped into the surf during the 1983 Labour Party Conference in Brighton. The rather embarassing image appeared repeatedly, especially in papers that oppose the Labour Party.

Trial by television

Media exposure (being constantly in the public eye) is a two-edged sword. Politicians and political parties often seem to think that 'any publicity is good publicity'. That is, exposure itself is the main concern and the actual content is not as important. Until the early 1960s, in Britain at least, political analysis was not at all threatening. Politicians would be 'lobbed' questions that only asked them where their party stood; the well-rehearsed reply would allow the politician to appear reasoned, wise and patriotic.

Things have changed since those days. Spurred on by the investigative reporting of Harold Evans's *Sunday Times* in the 1960s, and the way in which American reporters brought down President Richard Nixon in the Watergate scandal of the 1970s, political broadcasters now assume a far more sceptical and even inquisitorial role. Jeremy Paxman, one of the leading presenters of BBC 2's political programme 'Newsnight', explains this aggressive attitude: in conducting an interview, (usually with a high-level politician) he constantly thinks, 'Why is this person lying to me?'

A programme such as 'Any Questions' (Radio 4) or 'Question Time' (BBC 1) can be even more of a minefield – simply by letting the public get a word in! Polished political performers can often get by with a series of answers that avoid the issue on political programmes, but find it harder to 'duck and dive' when faced by a concerned member of the public. 'Question Time' has recognized this discomfort – and the public satisfaction in seeing it – in recent years, and has begun upsetting the political status quo by adding non-political people to its panel. Some observers have noted that such guests often act as 'loose cannons', expressing sentiments that their political counterparts would shy away from. Sometimes the politicians have been drawn further into the debate by accidentally following such a line of argument.

Democratic weapons – the role of satire

Laughter has been described as one of the most important weapons in a **democracy**. Political **satire**, aggressively pointing out the failings and hypocrisy of political leaders, has been a strong tradition within Britain. Sometimes the work of satirists even outlives the reputations of those being satirized. Some of the best television satire carries on the tradition. 'That Was the Week That Was' was the first example of TV satire, ridiculing both Government and opposition leaders in the early 1960s. 'Spitting Image' in the 1980s used grotesque caricature puppets to achieve the same ends. 'Have I Got News for You' combines comedy – often at the expense of well-known guests – with political satire.

FIND OUT...

Most newspapers carry political cartoons that take a satirical look at the day's events. Look at a range of newspapers on a particular day and see how their cartoons approach a particular issue.

THE KEY PLAYERS
Further afield

News wars

It could be hard for anyone outside Britain to understand how ITV's rescheduling of its flagship 'Ten O'clock News' could possibly have become a matter for intense debate in Parliament in late 2000. ITV decided to end the respected news programme, and schedule news at 6.30 in the evening instead. This would allow the station to show longer programmes and films in the evening without these being interrupted by the news. This would bring in more money from advertisers. Politicians were furious that the public could be denied their news because of such commercial considerations. ITV eventually responded to this pressure and reinstated the programme, by which time the BBC had moved their news programme to 10 o'clock.

Political interest in the media, like the above example, reflects the idea that broadcasting is a public service accountable to the people through Parliament.

Twin engines

Two themes emerging in the late 1980s formed the basis of the current range of broadcasting formats:

>> The first driving force was the rapid advance of new telecommunications technology, making it possible to beam television broadcasts off satellites in geostationary orbit. This opened up the possibility of broadcasting a vast number of programmes at the same time.

>> The second factor was political. New technology arrived just as the UK was in the middle of a prolonged spell of Conservative rule. Prime Minister Margaret Thatcher and her **Cabinet** strongly favoured competition, and it was this determination to open the broadcasting market that encouraged satellite broadcasting.

Responding to technology

The choice of satellite broadcasting in Britain today is dominated by BSkyB, which is owned by the News International media group. BSkyB exists because of a merger in the early 1990s of the original News International Sky with British Satellite Broadcasting (BSB), which received some government funding to help create competition. BSB, however, used technology that was ahead of its time and could not build satellite dishes fast enough.

Satellite television offers viewers a choice of standard channels (entertainment, sports, news and so on). The choice becomes more varied – and profitable for BSkyB – with the addition of direct pay subscription channels. Such channels are **encoded**, and can only be watched after viewers pay an additional fee to decode the signal.

One of the latest developments in the multiple-channel market is the system of **digital** compression broadcasting – digital television. Televisions in the future will be able to receive digital broadcasts directly; in the meantime, changing to digital is easier than it is to adapt to satellite broadcasting. The BBC is planning for an eventual expansion of **terrestrial** television channels using this technique. Digital services will initially be carried on six different transmission networks called **multiplexes.**

Across the UK, satellite dishes have become a common sight on houses and flats.

Multiplex operators

Each of the six digital multiplexes can carry a number of different television services at any one time; in total, about twenty new services will be available. The largest multiplex is able to reach around 90 per cent of the UK population, and the smallest around 70 per cent. Existing broadcasters operate two of the six multiplexes – the BBC operates one and the other is shared by ITV, Channel 4 and Teletext – who will all **simulcast** their existing services in digital form. They will use the additional capacity available to develop new digital services, such as BBC News 24 and FilmFour.

A third multiplex carries Channel 5, S4C (the Welsh language Channel 4) and a certain amount of Gaelic programming during peak hours in Scotland.

More of the same?

The explosion of new television channels should revolutionize the choice available to viewers. But in fact, the real choice could well become narrower over time.

With fewer restrictions on broadcasting 'home-grown' programming, satellite and digital broadcasters will be freer to show imported programmes as well as dozens of 'classic' repeats of old BBC and ITV favourites. Many media analysts predict that the BBC and ITV will 'dumb down' to compete with mass-market programming, leaving the viewer with far more choice – but of the same things.

THE KEY PLAYERS
Taken to task

Policing the press

Princes Charles and William – as well as Camilla Parker Bowles, Sir Paul McCartney, Noel Gallagher and Meg Mathews, George Michael and Julie Goodyear – turned up on 7 February 2001 for the tenth birthday party of the Press Complaints Commission (PCC). The PCC, which acts as a watchdog against press excesses, and most of the guests had had reason to complain about intrusive or misleading press coverage in the past year.

Most agree that the Press Complaints Commission succeeds. Its success in getting 'justice' for the rich and famous sometimes hides its more central role in serving the public interest and ending practices such as 'chequebook journalism' (paying large sums for exclusive rights to criminal stories).

Other watchdogs

The success of the PCC has helped to give more power to similar watchdogs working in the broadcasting industry. Like the PCC, these are non-governmental bodies with responsibilities for maintaining high standards and sorting out complaints. The umbrella organization is the Broadcasting Standards Commission (BSC), which began operating in 1997. It has a legal duty to investigate complaints about unfairness and invasions of privacy in all forms of broadcasting in the UK (radio and TV, BBC and commercial stations). Broadcasters are expected to comply with the codes that the BSC has developed.

This is the petrol station in Gibraltar where the British SAS shot dead three IRA bombing suspects in 79, seen as a still from the ITV documentary 'Death on the Rock'. The programme called into question a possible 'shoot to kill' policy, leading the Conservative government of the time to complain bitterly to the ITC about political bias.

Complaints directed at any BBC broadcasts, either radio or television, are dealt with by the BBC Governors' Programme Complaints Appeals Committee. The Independent TV Commission (ITC) performs a similar function for all commercial TV broadcasting (**terrestrial**, satellite and cable) in the UK.

Making a complaint

Members of the public can criticize an article appearing in the press or a programme broadcast on either television or radio. Below are the main bodies responsible for controlling different branches of the media.

>> Press Complaints Commission: It expects the person complaining to have made an initial approach to the editor of the offending publication and to lodge their complaint within one month of the article appearing or the last letter received from the editor. If the matter is not resolved, the Commission will make its own judgement. If the person complaining is successful, the publication is under a (moral) obligation to publish the PCC's ruling, which is also published in the PCC's quarterly reports. There is no compensation.

>> Broadcasting Standards Commission: Any viewer or listener may complain about any programme, but they are expected to do so in writing within two months of a TV broadcast or three weeks of a radio broadcast. If the complaint is not resolved through verbal or written communication the BSC may hold a formal hearing. If the BSC finds in your favour the broadcaster will have to publish a correction and apology on the airwaves and in a publication of your choice.

>> ITC: Any person making a complaint is expected to supply details of the offending programme (title, when it was broadcast and by which company) and a summary of their complaint. The Commission may require broadcasters to publish on-screen apologies and corrections.

>> Radio Authority: The Radio Authority accepts complaints from members of the public, who are expected to make their views known to the offending station first. If a complaint is upheld, the Authority may require the station to broadcast an apology or correction.

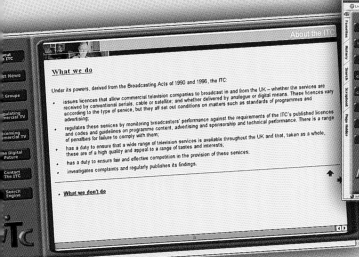

Back   Forward   Reload   Home

THE KEY PLAYERS
The Internet

The biggest development in communications technology in the 1990s and beyond has been the rise of the Internet. This worldwide linking of computers, using **modems** to transfer information along telephone lines, has meant that someone sitting in front of a computer in a Somerset village can book a hotel room in Las Vegas, buy the latest best-selling book or have flowers delivered to Sydney – all with the click of a mouse.

Wider access to the Internet – both in individual households and for schools – has been one of the goals of the Labour Party since its election victory in May 1997. Electronic communications analysts reckon that the UK is about five years behind the United States in its use of the Internet. This suggests that American Internet-based companies could race even further ahead in securing world markets. However, it means that the UK can learn from some of the mistakes that have occurred in the United States. The 'dot.com crash' of 2000–2001, during which share prices of hundreds of Web-based companies plunged, is one of the economic problems which Britain might be able to avoid. In the meantime the problem of access remains. Despite increasing competition from Internet Service Providers (ISPs), phone charges remain higher in the UK than in other developed countries.

The information superhighway

The Internet was developed in 1973 as part of a project sponsored by the United States Department of Defense Advanced Research Projects Agency (ARPA). It began as a computer network of ARPA (ARPAnet) that linked computer networks at several universities and research laboratories in the United States. At that point the Internet was still seen as mainly an American project, and it had very little publicity outside the United States, except in specialist computer engineering circles.

Things changed in 1989, and it was a British computer scientist who really introduced the potential of the Internet to the world. The World Wide Web was developed in 1989 by English computer scientist Timothy Berners-Lee for the

>>

European Organization for Nuclear Research (CERN). It was only then that the dream of an 'information superhighway' began to form. The 'Web' offered a **democratic** – some say **anarchic** – method of spreading information.

E-mail

Electronic mail, or e-mail, has grown rapidly as a means of communication in the last few years, starting out as a handy alternative to faxing and evolving into a clever way of sending large text or image files as attachments to mail messages. Apart from the obvious risks of transporting computer viruses, e-mail has created huge debate about privacy infringement. The Government has made suggestions about monitoring e-mails of individuals and corporations as way of collecting evidence in criminal trials. This has provoked angry responses, especially from newspapers and periodicals that rely on the confidentiality of their information.

Untapped resources

In its brief history, the Internet has had its share of shocks, notably the unstable performance of many Web-based companies. But the Internet itself is unlikely to be affected by these events, because of its versatility and its fast means of communicating. On-line forums and chat rooms are popular because they enable users to talk to dozens of other Internet users. Also, since anyone can set up a

Timothy Berners-Lee, developer of the World Wide Web, remains a passionate campaigner for cyber-communication.

Web page, the Internet represents true media democracy.

The Internet is also capable of sending, storing and displaying a wide variety of files in many different formats. For example, until February 2001 it was possible to log on to the Napster.com website and download music for free. Films can be sent and viewed – the only limitation is download time. But even there, the new **digital** technology might have an answer, in the form of the **integrated services digital network (ISDN)**. This network will be able to transmit all kinds of data around the world in digital form, through a variety of media and at very high speeds.

The Internet and Government

Anyone with a personal computer now has access to far more information than in the 1980s. While many feel that Governments have been slow to understand the power of the World Wide Web, they are now making more information available. All Government departments have websites and the UK's citizens have access to information that was previously only available through the traditional media or organizations such as public libraries.

FIND OUT... 🔍 >>

The main Government website can be found at www.ukonline.gov.uk The site has a number of Government related links, all different aspects of Government, as well as regional topics.

Compose a mail message

THE KEY PLAYERS
Media moguls

Manipulating information for political reasons is, in its most extreme form, called propaganda. The United Kingdom, the United States and Australia – all members of the **free press** – have engaged in propaganda over and over again. Usually, the control of the news has been understandable and more or less accepted by the public, especially during times of war. More controversially, governments have also controlled the news during peacetime. In these circumstances, they find themselves criticized by civil liberties groups, as well as by powerful voices outside government.

But imagine being able to use such power on a personal level. In effect, that is what the influential and powerful group known as 'media **moguls**' is able to do. This group includes people such as Rupert Murdoch, Ted Turner of CNN and – slightly differently – Microsoft's Bill Gates. Control (in this case, ownership) over one medium, such as print journalism, means that news stories can be given a personal or political angle. In the case of these modern moguls, with their fingers in several media 'pies', the scope for influencing the media is immense.

Pushing the boundaries

With satellite television and the Internet already 'leapfrogging' the boundaries of countries, it is possible to see how concentrated ownership (financial control over communications media in the hands of a few) could build into international empires. Microsoft, the huge US software **corporation** (with Bill Gates, one of the world's richest people, as its principal shareholder) has been stopped from imposing a Microsoft **browser** as the main software tool for navigating the Internet.

It is in the field of satellite television, with its ability to bypass some national restrictions, that Rupert Murdoch spreads his wings. With special offers for satellite dishes or favourable reviews of satellite broadcasting appearing in his range of News International newspapers, Murdoch is able to use one medium to boost sales in another.

Greenpeace and other campaigning groups have websites that often target major corporations – including those trying to control the Internet itself.

The case for concentration

Although there is widespread concern about the concentration of media ownership in the hands of a few individuals or corporations, governments have been prepared to accept many of the arguments in favour of such concentration. The debate about the desirability or even the **ethics** of narrow-based ownership continues, but below are some of the main arguments that defend such a system – broad ideals such as freedom, **democracy**, progress and initiative. Hand in hand with the arguments for concentration are calls for less governmental regulation to restrain these rights.

>> **Pluralism**: There is an explosion of choice and diversity in the media – pluralism is secured – there is no need to keep regulations designed to bring about pluralism either externally (through ownership regulation) or internally (public service broadcasting, effective codes for journalistic integrity and so on).

> *(Owning newspapers brings me) a little smidgen of power. That's the fun of it, isn't it?*
>
> **(Rupert Murdoch, quoted in *The Penguin Book of Journalism*)**

FIND OUT... >>

Rupert Murdoch's News Corporation owns a huge number of media companies. Visit their website (www.newscorp.com) to find out the names of these companies and what they do.

>> Media democracy: New media (especially the Internet) are leading to a transformation of media power and of democracy – the technologies themselves have a democratic potential which will replace the old media structures and institutions and enable forms of **direct democracy** to triumph. Further restraints on ownership are unnecessary.

>> Competition and **consumer welfare**: The sort of economic approach favoured by conservatives around the world believes that competition and competitiveness are encouraged by a market system, and actually increase consumer welfare. So, restrictions represent unacceptable government interference in the market.

>> Global competitiveness: Firms need to be larger to compete globally. Since 1994, European policy has been dominated by an argument that regulatory restrictions should be relaxed so that large firms can be created more easily. These firms should be allowed to generate profits from the commercial development of new media services, because they might then invest in **network infrastructure**, improving factors such as employment and education.

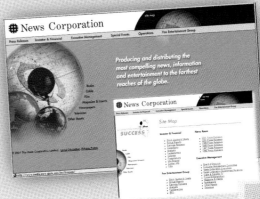

BRITAIN'S ROLE
Regional awareness

Matching the progress of the information revolution in the United Kingdom almost step by step has been the ideological battle over 'Europe'. This debate – sometimes centring on political affairs and at other times economic – has had side effects in nearly every aspect of British society.

Federalism and the regions

The battle to 'save the pound' rather than adopt the Euro currency is linked to a feeling that the United Kingdom is being edged into joining a 'United States of Europe'. The most distasteful word to anti-Europe campaigners is **federalism** – the linking of federated states into a wider 'group'. 'Britishness', they argue, would be lost under such an arrangement. But within Britain itself, since the Labour party victory in 1997, there have been moves towards a sort of federalism. The new Scottish Parliament, along with the new assemblies in Wales and Northern Ireland, has highlighted just how regional Britain itself is.

Beyond the framework of regions is the concern about the ethnic and social nature of each part of the nation as a whole. We

Alf Young **on the unspoken fear haunting Labour. Plus** Appointments **and** Motori

The Herald

EST 1783

GLASGOW

219th year No 96

Friday May 18, 2001

Baby, I'm fed up pretending

Features, Page 18

Lomu the Barbarian

Sport, Page 34

Gordon's black sp

INTERVIEW Page 2

Revealed: the first Scottish painting to be bought by the National Gallery in London

Prescott is given special protection

shadow deputy PM rty closes ranks after punch

tims of egg-throwing yesterday.

now live in a society in which it has become easier to move about – both in search of employment, and in a social sense. The same period has seen wide scale immigration, with waves of people arriving from the Caribbean, South Asia and more recently, as asylum seekers from war-torn Europe.

Addressing the regions

The press has been the traditional means of representing and reflecting regional interests. Like the press overall in Britain, regional newspapers and periodicals developed within the private sector, free of government interference, but forced to live or die by the advertising and **circulation** revenue they create. Some of the leading newspapers, such as the *Scotsman* and the *Western Mail*, are papers of record, meaning that they are frequently quoted for their views on regional and national affairs. The vast majority – numbering about 120 Sunday papers and 2000 dailies – are more concerned with local news, however. The past two decades have seen a rise in **freesheets**; local papers that are free and rely completely on advertising revenue.

Broadcasting also shows a rich regional diversity. The BBC operates 39 local radio stations as well as regional radio services in Scotland, Wales and Northern Ireland. These stations must provide and reflect the ethnic diversity of the region. Local news bulletins appear on BBC 1 television, and the same network (BBC 1) has regional programme variations in Northern Ireland, Scotland and Wales. The bidding framework of the ITV **franchises** has a built-in local bias. Each of the fifteen programming companies broadcast to (and in much of the programming, concentrate on) the fifteen local regions. In addition, S4C (linked to Channel 4) broadcasts in Wales, giving special emphasis to Welsh-language programmes and other matters of Welsh concern.

The role of radio

Local radio has been vital in reflecting regional identity as well as providing programming geared to ethnic minorities within each of these regions. BBC local radio is committed to giving England's multi-racial and multi-lingual groups a voice in the community. BBC local radio stations across England broadcast nearly 150 hours of ethnic material each week.

One of the most successful local radio initiatives is actually a collective of several stations in the Midlands, a region that has traditionally supported a large immigrant population. The Midlands Asian Network broadcasts 70 hours a week on BBC Radio WM, Radio Leicester, and BBC CWR (Coventry and Warwickshire Radio). The mix of programming includes news and current affairs from Britain and abroad, phone-in programmes tackling Asian social problems, helplines and music from classical Indian to the Eastern pop music Bhangra. These programmes are mainly in English, but increasingly popular are 'mother tongue' news broadcasts in Hindi, Urdu and Bengali, provided by the BBC World Service.

Left: *The Herald* **is one of Scotland's most influential broadsheet newspapers.**

BRITAIN'S ROLE
Northern Ireland - a special case?

The 'Irish Question' has been a thorn in the side of British Governments for many years. Since the island of Ireland was divided in the early 1920s, leaving six of its 32 counties as part of the United Kingdom, the British and Irish people have tried to come to terms with a political situation that is unique in recent British history.

Northern Ireland is the only part of the United Kingdom where British troops have been used, and where UK forces have faced a determined and often violent opposition in the form of the Irish Republican Army (IRA) and other **paramilitary** groups. Since the late 1990s, however, a more optimistic attitude has existed in Northern Ireland. The Governments of the UK and the Republic of Ireland – and more importantly the Northern Irish people themselves – have tried to forge a new society in which two conflicting traditions can live together in peace.

Emotive words

The 'special case' nature of Northern Ireland has given it unique status in terms of domestic news reporting in the United Kingdom. Over the years there have been serious questions about Government interference, political bias and getting rid of basic rights such as free speech. Even the vocabulary used in reporting is affected. What seem at first glance to be straightforward terms are often seen by one of the sides (broadly speaking Unionist and Nationalist) as opinionated or politically controversial. The very term 'Northern Ireland' is avoided by many Nationalists, who prefer phrases such as 'the Six Counties' or simply 'the North'. Similar terms that cause anger include 'Sinn Fein/IRA' (used by Unionists to link Sinn Fein with terrorism), 'the Mainland' (referring to the island of Great Britain and shunned by Nationalists) and 'Derry' (the Nationalist preference over 'Londonderry'). Even the term 'peace process' stirs up resentment from many Unionists, who see it simply as a series of concessions that will inevitably lead to a united Ireland.

Although often termed 'Ulster', Northern Ireland in fact comprises only six of Ulster's nine counties. The other three are part of the Republic of Ireland.

The role of the Government

The 'Troubles' in Northern Ireland flared up into full-scale conflict in 1969, and in the decades leading to the Good Friday Agreement of 1998 (which paved the way for many new institutions such as the Northern Ireland Assembly), the war of words was as important as the peacekeeping role of the military.

The Northern Ireland Information Service (NIIS) is the public relations branch of the Northern Ireland Office. The NIIS uses its large budget (it spent £7.2 million in 1989–90) to write positive stories about Northern Ireland, which are given to the world's media without charge and free of **copyright** restrictions. The London Radio Service of the Central Office of Information similarly 'places' stories (usually ministerial speeches and features), but the station broadcasts the material as if it were its own.

As well as providing selective information, the Government also acted to stem the flow of information from Northern Ireland. From 1988 the Government banned the broadcasting of direct statements by representatives or supporters of eleven Irish political and military organizations (most notably Sinn Fein and the IRA). The ban was only lifted in 1994 after the Government decided that some of these organizations were important elements in the early peace process.

Gerry Adams and Sinn Fein colleagues hold a press conference in Dublin in 2000 before meetings on the Good Friday Agreement with the Irish Prime Minister.

Dangerous reporting

The Official Secrets Act (see pages 38–39) is normally seen as a deterrent, steering reporters away from giving out sensitive information. But typically, it was only in the tense media climate surrounding Northern Ireland that the Act has been used recently in the courts. Tony Geraghty became the first British journalist to be charged in 22 years under the Act. Police and detectives raided Geraghty's home in December 1998 after he refused to remove what Ministry of Defence officials claimed was 'damaging material' from a paperback version of his book, *The Irish War*. A year later, charges against him were finally dropped. Both before and after being charged, Geraghty said he had been subjected to 'a process of consistent harassment, pressure and bullying' for writing about how intelligence agencies had used computer surveillance in Northern Ireland.

BRITAIN'S ROLE
Whose information?

It has often been said that news gathering in Britain takes place within a 'climate of secrecy'. Freedom of the press (and of all media) is a cherished tradition, but the flow of information through the press and to the general public is often carefully controlled. These controls act on both official and unofficial levels, and some of them have been in place since the end of the nineteenth century.

The most significant restraint on media access to information is the Official Secrets Act. The Act came into being in 1911, three years before the start of the First World War. At the time, Britain was preoccupied with what was seen to be threatening behaviour by the Germans. Parliament responded with the passing of the Official Secrets Act as a means of preventing **espionage**. The Act was revised in 1989, but its basic 'rules' are largely the same: vast amounts of Government information is considered to be 'off limits' to the media, and particularly sensitive defence-related items are even more strictly controlled under what are called D-Notices. Reporters must find much of their news about the Government through official channels such as the ministerial press offices. Coupled with these methods of reporting, there is the less official Lobby System (see pages 14–15), which was established in 1884.

Former MI5 security officer, David Shayler, and his girlfriend speak to reporters and supporters after he was released on bail. He was charged with breaking the Official Secrets Act after he spoke to the press about allegations of British Secret Service incompetence.

New openings?

Not every country operates the same system of controlling information. The United States, Ireland, New Zealand, the Netherlands and even the formerly communist government of Hungary are among the states that have Freedom of Information Acts. Such legislation lessens the amount of 'off limits' information considerably, isolating only information that can rightly be considered harmful to defence, national security or law and order. A non-political organization known as the Campaign for Freedom of Information has been pressing for similar legislation in Britain for nearly twenty years.

The Labour Government was elected in May 1997 and promised 'We are pledged to a Freedom of Information Act'. In December 1997 it published a **white paper**, *Your Right to Know*, setting out its proposals. In May 1999 it published a draft Freedom of Information Bill for further consultation. In December 1999 the Government introduced its Freedom of Information Bill into the House of Commons. The Bill has yet to be used, and critics argue that it does not go far enough.

Tangled Web

One of the areas of greatest concern for anti-censorship activists is the World Wide Web and its associated software possibilities, such as e-mail attachments, Web browsing and tracing downloaded information. Like so many topics trying to find a balance between national security, public safety and the free flow of information, 'e-policing' has stirred up strong emotions.

In 2000, Britain was experiencing some of its most aggressive anti-paedophile campaigns. The public supported the police when it was disclosed that a number of paedophiles (someone who sexually abuses children) had been convicted using evidence from computer intervention – linked to downloaded Internet information. This represented a dramatic new development in evidence-gathering techniques and few people championed the civil rights of the accused. However, in May 2000, the *Guardian* and its sister paper the *Observer* wrote that MI5 (the Government intelligence service) 'is reported to be building a new £25 million pound surveillance system... to monitor e-mails and other Internet messages sent and received in Britain.' That report followed a London judge's order that the *Guardian* and *Observer* newspapers hand over any e-mails or notes relating to a former MI5 security officer, David Shayler, who leaked confidential information. The newspapers are appealing the ruling.

> ❛(It is) remarkably difficult to purge an e-mail...When we first had warning that the Government would come after us ... I thought I had managed to purge every e-mail in the system, and then found there was some backup copy to a backup copy.❜
>
> (*Guardian* editor Alan Rusbridger, referring to a story concerning former MI5 security officer David Shayler, June 2000)

PART 5

LOOK TO THE FUTURE
Confusion or clarity ?

Reporting on the move

Massive public demonstrations forced President Joseph Estrada of the Philippines out of office in January 2001. International reporters were on the scene, trying to tap into the quickly changing mood of the crowd in Manila. They, or others like them, had covered fast-breaking stories like this one for decades. The reporters' refrain during such events was usually 'Have you got enough film?' or 'Do you know where the nearest phone is?'. In 2001 it was different: 'Is your mobile charged?'

Estrada's fall was certainly captured on film, and some reporters did find 'land line' telephones to file their stories. But the most important reporting tool this time was the mobile phone. Apart from being able to phone or e-mail their offices from the middle of the action, reporters were able to exchange text messages with each other – and with the demonstrators themselves – as the events unfolded. Many Filipinos were similarly equipped, which helped blur the distinction between planning, participation and reporting.

Domestic freedom

The Philippine experience – for both participants and reporters – was a perfect example of the modern media age with all its complexities and potential. On one level it was 'business as usual'. A news story was being reported and readers and viewers in far-off countries eventually saw the events unfold. But on another level, it demonstrated the blurring of boundaries between different types of communications, and it is this blurring that will affect all of us in the future.

Follow the report of one of those print journalists back to his or her offices in Britain, and you would see how things really have changed, even since the 1990s. The traditional job roles of reporter, typesetter and printer are gone. Text can be put directly on to computer screens, images scanned and dropped in next to the text and the whole article made ready for publication within minutes.

This blurring of distinctions extends to our households. The computer has become an indispensable tool for processing and finding out information. And with the Web, it has taken over some of the roles of other forms of communication. The 90-second trailer for the 'Harry Potter' film, was first broadcast on the Internet 1 March 2001, and not on television or in cinemas.

The process can move from one screen to another. Many analysts expect that most British households will be equipped with interactive televisions within a decade or so. These sets will receive **terrestrial**, satellite or cable broadcasts, but their 'interactivity' will enable them to be used as Internet

> **'**Promoting effective competition is complex in an environment where technology means that a vast array of new services is being offered to consumers – from video-conferencing and e-commerce, to distance learning and remote teaching; from e-banking and home shopping to television on demand and interactive games; from telemedicine to teleworking; and e-Government with huge potential applications.**'**
>
> (Quoted from a paper by the Director-General of Telecommunications, July 2000)

US President George W Bush as a candidate on the campaign trail in 2000. Many fear that British General Elections could soon resemble those in the United States where image and **sound bites** are all-important.

terminals as well. Suddenly the prospect of infinite choice – far greater than what was promised by the advent of satellite broadcasting – has become much more real. Films and other programmes will be downloaded, and people will be able to bank or shop on the Internet at the same time as watching these films.

Virtual reality, real control?

Many people find the loss of age-old ideas, opinions and ways of life invigorating. On a personal level, even a decade from now people will laugh at our attempts to type up large quantities of information: voice-activated computers may be the norm by then. And the many possibilities of virtual reality technology will no doubt enter the world of the media, rather than just be restricted to the field of entertainment. Consumers in 2030 will not just read about governments toppling, or watch them on the screen. They will be able to experience the events themselves, mingling with the rioting and the wounded. The prospect is exciting on one level, but on another it shows some of the dangers lying in wait. Existing laws and regulations help monitor what we read or watch, and the press and broadcasting media are largely accountable to the public. But who will be there to decide what we actually experience in future decades, and how will we know what is real? That is the real challenge for the future.

DEBATE
Issues for discussion

This book has introduced a number of topics that are controversial. The history of the media in Britain has been full of complexities, contradictions, Government interventions and public reactions. Sometimes it takes a 'media event' such as the funeral of the Princess of Wales in 1997, for the country to take stock of itself. And with the boundaries of the media becoming increasingly difficult to define, it is worth examining some of the questions that Britain faces as it enters the new millennium.

Is there a case for concentrated ownership of media resources?

>> Is it a bad thing that individuals, such as Rupert Murdoch and Bill Gates – or their respective **corporations** News Corporation and Microsoft – should be able to own such a large share of the expanding media world?

>> How do the arguments put forward by such **moguls** – in favour of market and competition-driven development – stand up?

Can – and should – the Internet be monitored and regulated more closely?

Both the strengths and weaknesses of the Internet, more specifically the World Wide Web, lie in its lack of overall control and structure.

>> Can the spirit of Web **democracy** – seen in individual home pages and the free flow of ideas – survive any regulation?

>> What about information that is racially or sexually offensive, and which would not be allowed in the print or broadcast media?

>> And if we do allow some regulation, where do we draw the line?

Who should decide what constitutes 'national interest' in the field of the media?

Journalists in Britain have traditionally been constrained by the limits imposed by the Official Secrets Act, and other Government legislation that prevents disclosure of information that might be damaging to the national interests. But many media analysts have argued that such restrictions have themselves been harmful to the national interest by denying the public the chance to discuss and think about controversial issues. Has the existence of Freedom of Information Acts in countries such as the United States, Ireland and New Zealand led to a dangerous lack of national morals, or have such Acts strengthened these countries by leading to a better-informed public?

Is the present system of political broadcast advertising the best way of informing the British voters?

>> Would the public be better served if political parties were more easily able to pay for party political statements, as is the case in the United States and some other countries?

>> Do voters learn more by being exposed to a greater level of such advertising, or does the advertising simply lead to a 'cash race' to see which party can afford the most extensive advertising campaign?

>> Or if the present British system is preferable, does it deny smaller parties a fair share of air time?

Do ethnic and other minorities play a large enough role in creating the agenda for Britain's media?

>> Does the 'look' of the BBC and ITV accurately reflect the rich ethnic diversity of Britain as a whole?

It can seem embarrassing, or even shameful, to look back at broadcasting of the 1970s and 1980s in order to see how black people, Asians or homosexuals were portrayed.

>> Would observers from 2020 be equally appalled by today's choice of programming?

>> And do minority groups figure prominently enough in presenting and reporting the news itself?

Should media regulators be part of the Government itself?

Most people seem satisfied with, or unconcerned by, the way in which the various bodies looking after British media interests are made up. These groups have been established by Parliament and must abide by statutory requirements, but their members are mainly appointed.

>> Would elected representatives, who would be more accountable to the public, be more effective in this role, or would such a system lead to far too much government interference and control?

Should special sporting events always remain 'free to air'?

Major events such as the FA Cup, Wimbledon and the Olympics have remained the preserve of the 'free to air' branch of broadcasting, the BBC and ITV.

>> But in the current climate of commercial competition, does this system work against the interests of the public by denying the right of satellite and other subscription services to bid for these rights?

FURTHER RESOURCES

The subject of the media in the United Kingdom is diverse and constantly changing. Below are listed some useful and informative books, addresses and Web sites relating to this fascinating area. There are contact addresses and Web links for professional and regulatory bodies dealing with the media. These organizations not only provide information about working conditions and standards within the industry, but they also have useful advice about starting a career in the media.

Umbrella and regulatory media organizations

Advertising Standards Authority

2 Torrington Place, London WC1E 7HW

Tel: 020 7580 5555, Fax: 020 7631 3051

Website: www.asa.org.uk

The ASA deals with complaints about newspaper and magazine advertisements.

BBC Information Office

Tel: 020 8743 8000 (for TV)

Tel: 020 7580 4468 (for radio)

Tel: 020 8576 8988 (Minicom number for the deaf)

This office deals with telephoned comments, queries or criticisms from the general public.

Broadcasting Standards Commission

7 The Sanctuary, London SW1P 3JS

Tel: 020 7222 3172, Fax: 020 7233 0544

Website: www.bsc.org.uk

The BSC handles complaints about breach of privacy or unjust or unfair treatment on radio or television.

Independent Television Commission (ITC)

33 Foley Street, London W1P 7LB

Tel: 020 7255 3000, Fax: 020 7306 7800

Website: http://www.itc.org.uk

The ITC is the public body responsible for licensing and regulating commercially funded television services provided in and from the UK. These include Channel 3 (ITV), Channel 4, Channel 5 and a range of cable, local delivery and satellite services.

Press Complaints Commission

1 Salisbury Square, London EC4 8AE

Tel: 020 7353 1284, Fax: 020 7353 8355

Website: www.pcc.org.uk

The PCC deals with complaints about newspapers and magazines. It also upholds a Code of Practice and advises editors on journalistic ethics.

Radio Authority

Holbrook House, 14 Great Queen Street

London WC2B 5DG,

Tel: 020 7430 2724 Fax: 020 7405 7064

Website: www.radioauthority.org.uk

The Radio Authority handles all complaints about independent radio within the United Kingdom.

Campaigning organizations

Campaign for Freedom of Information

Suite 102, 16 Baldwins Gardens, London EC1N 7RJ

Tel: 020 7831 7477, Fax: 020 7831 7461

Website: www.cfoi.org.uk

The Campaign for Freedom of Information (CFOI) is a multi-party organization pressing for more open government in the United Kingdom, especially through the creation of a Freedom of Information Bill.

Press Wise

25 Easton Business Centre, Felix Road, Bristol BS5 0HE

Tel: 0117 941 5889, Fax: 0117 941 5848

E-mail: pw@presswise.org.uk

Website: www.presswise.org.uk

Press Wise is a non-profit-making organization promoting high standards of journalism, and aiming to give power to ordinary people who become victims of unfair media intrusion and inaccurate or irresponsible reporting.

Media unions and professional bodies

Broadcasting, Entertainment, Cinematographer and Theatre Union (BECTU)

111 Wardour Street, London W1V 4AY

Tel: 020 7437 8506, Fax: 020 7437 8258

Email: bectu@bectu.org.uk

Website: www.bectu.org.uk

BECTU is the main trade union for workers in broadcasting, film, theatre and other sectors of the entertainment and media industry.

Communication Workers Union

150 Brunswick Road, London W5 1AW

Tel: 020 8998 2981, Fax: 020 8991 1410

E-mail: 101513.1054@compuserve.com

Website: www.cwu.org

This is the largest trade union in posts, telecommunications and financial services.

European Federation of Journalists

Rue Royale, 266, B1210 Brussels, Belgium

Tel 0032 2 223 2265, E-mail: efj@pophost.eunet.be

Website: www.ifj.org/jetpilot

The European Federation of Journalists is a European project designed to help develop an ethical approach to the training of journalists in aspects of on-line and digital media, under the stated aim of 'Putting journalism standards first'.

Musenet - Media Unions Information Society and Education Network

c/o The Labour Telematics Centre, GMB National College

College Road, Manchester M16 8BP

Tel: 0161 860 4364, Fax: 0161 881 1853

E-mail: info@labourtel.org.uk

Website: www.ifj.org/musenet/

Musenet is a jointly operated media union information network that aims to provide the public and aspiring media workers with detailed and accurate news about the media in the United Kingdom.

National Union of Journalists

Acorn House, 314–320 Grays Inn Road
London WC1N 3XX

Tel: 020 7278 7916, Fax: 020 7278 6617

E-mail: acorn.house@nuj.org.uk

Website: www.nuj.org.uk

The NUJ is the leading trade union representing all editorial sections of the media, including photographers and freelancers. Membership totals 29,000 including 1,800 student members.

Writers Guild of Great Britain

430 Edgeware Road, London W2 1EH

Tel: 020 7723 8074, Fax: 020 7706 2413

E-mail: postie@wggb.demon.co.uk

The Writers Guild of Great Britain is the trade union representing professional writers in film, TV, radio, theatre and books.

Further reading

The Mass Media and Power in Modern Britain, by John Eldridge, Jenny Kitzinger and Kevin Williams; Oxford: Oxford University Press, 1997.

The Penguin Book of Journalism, edited by Stephen Glover; London: Penguin Books, 1999.

Ruling Britannia (The Failure and Future of British Democracy), by Andrew Marr; London: Michael Joseph, 1995.

GLOSSARY

anarchy, anarchic   lacking in any formal system of organization

authoritarian   accepting or permitting little or no dispute

broadsheet   a large-format newspaper containing more pages than a tabloid and usually allowing its writers more space for analysis

browser   a software tool for navigating through the Internet

Cabinet   the group of ministers who meet regularly to decide on government policy under the chairmanship of the Prime Minister

circulation   the amount of paid copies of a newspaper or magazine, either sold or sent to subscribers

consensus   broad agreement, usually among a large number of people

consumer welfare   the public good, in particular relating to safety and fair trading

copyright   the exclusive right to make copies of an image or piece of writing

corporation   a legally based association of individuals that has powers and responsibilities that are different from those of its members

democracy, democratic   a political system of government that allows voters to express opinion and choose representatives.

deregulation   reducing the number of regulations and other legal obstacles standing in the way of commercial operations

desks   in newspaper terms, departments such as Sport, Home News, International

digital   relating to a system that allows terrestrial transmitters, as well as satellites, to broadcast a number of multiple programmes on a single frequency

direct democracy   a political system that enables voters to have an immediate say

duopoly   two individuals or companies that together have a monopoly over the sale of particular good or services

encapsulating   presenting complicated information in a clear and easily understood fashion

encoded   having information deliberately jumbled to prevent unauthorized people from recieving it in a clear fashion

espionage   organized spying, usually on behalf of another country

ethics   a socially agreed system of right and wrong

federalism   the linking of federated states or other political bodies within a wider united whole

franchise   the commercial right to operate in a certain area or region

free press   a system that prevents the government from interfering in printed (the press) and other media

freesheets   newspapers or other periodicals that are delivered for free

geostationary   orbiting the Earth at the same speed - and in the same direction - as the Earth's rotation, keeping it over the same point on Earth at all times

highbrow	catering to the needs and preferences of well-educated or intelligent people
integrated services digital network (ISDN)	a high-speed system of sending information through a variety of media in digital form
libel	a written untruth about an individual or group of individuals
low-power stations	early radio stations that only had enough power to broadcast locally
modems	equipment that allows a computer to be linked to other computers via telephone lines
moguls	a term for an Indian ruler, used informally to refer to powerful owners of newspapers or broadcasting companies
monopoly	the chance to sell a product or service without competition from other individuals or companies
multiplexes	any of the six different transmission networks carrying digital television services
network infrastructures	the practical workings of a system linking different types of media
paramilitary	operating as an unofficial military force
parchment	the skin of sheep or goats prepared for use as a material on which to write
periodical	a magazine published at regular intervals
plaintiff	the person who brings a charge against someone else (the defendant) in a court of law
pluralist, pluralism	diversity and variety, usually used as a goal
proprietors	the owners and managers of commercial businesses such as newspapers or magazines
Puritan	a member of the Church of England in the sixteenth century who favoured simple forms of worship
redress	a form of compensation, sometimes in the form of money
Reformation	the period beginning in the early sixteenth century when Christians questioned and opposed the authority of the Roman Catholic Church and returned to a more Biblical emphasis in worship
Renaissance	the period in European history (roughly from the fourteenth to sixteenth centuries) when art and culture rediscovered ancient methods and used them in tandem with new views about human potential
satire, satirical	using humour, irony or ridicule to reveal the bad points of a person or issue
simulcast	silmultaneous transmission on different television channels
sound bite	an easily remembered political phrase consisting of only a few words
stakeholder	someone who has a stake in the performance and delivery of a service in society
tabloid	a small-format newspaper usually (but not always) concentrating more on entertainment and less on analysis than a broadsheet
terrestrial	land-based (in broadcasting terms used to distinguish it from satellite-based)
victuallers	someone who furnishes food or provisions
wavelengths	the rate at which radio or television signal is received, usually marked out for a single station
white paper	an official document outlining government policy

INDEX

advertising   16, 19

BBC   5,11, 18–19, 20–3, 27, 35

Broadcasting Standards Commission   28, 29

broadsheets   12, 13, 14, 17, 46

censorship   17

Church, the   6, 7, 8

competition   22–3, 33

complaints   28–9

consumer welfare   33, 46

corrants   8

debates   42–3

democracy   4, 25, 31, 33, 42, 46

deregulation   22, 46

'desks'   14

digital technology   27, 31, 46

e-mail   31, 39

editors   14

eighteenth century   10–11

ethics   17

ethnic diversity   35, 43

Europe   34

Fleet Street   11

franchises   19, 35, 46

free press   9, 12, 32, 46

freedom of information   39, 42

freesheets   16, 35, 46

Government   8, 15, 18, 31, 36, 37, 43

history   6–11

income sources   16, 19

Independent Television Commission   11, 19, 22, 29

information control   38–9, 42

Internet   4, 5, 30–1, 32, 39, 40, 42

ITV   22–3, 26

Labour Party   4, 22, 30, 39

law, the   17, 18, 37, 38, 39, 42

magazines   13

Maxwell, Robert   17

'media moguls'   32, 47

Middle Ages   6

monopolies   11, 19

multiplex operators   27, 47

Murdoch, Rupert   17, 32, 33, 42

Northern Ireland   36–7

Official Secrets Act   37, 38, 39, 42

ownership   16–17, 32, 33, 42

parchment   7, 47

Philippines   40

pluralism   33, 47

political broadcasting   24, 25, 43

press briefings   15

Press Complaints Commission   17, 28, 29

printing press   7, 8

Private Eye   13, 17

publicity, TV   24–5

Puritan movement   8, 47

radio   11, 18, 20, 21, 35

Radio Authority   21, 29

Reformation   8, 47

regions   34, 35

Reith, John   11, 19

religious documents   6–7

Renaissance   8, 47

resources   44–5

satellites   26, 27, 32, 41

satire   25

scribes   6–7

'sound bites'   24, 47

stakeholders   5, 47

Sunday newspapers   11, 13

tabloids   12, 13, 14, 17, 47

television   11, 18, 22–7, 41

United States   30

virtual reality   41

Walter, John   10

watchdogs   28

World Service   20

Titles in the *Citizen's Guide* series include:

Hardback   0 431 14493 1

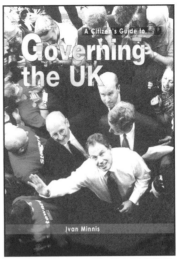

Hardback   0 431 14492 3

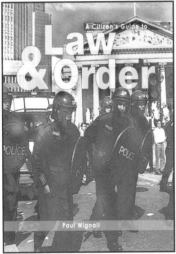

Hardback   0 431 14495 8

Hardback   0 431 14491 5

Hardback   0 431 14494 X

Hardback   0 431 14490 7

Find out about the other titles in this series on our website www.heinemann.co.uk/library